The Oxford Treasury of Christmas Poems

OXFORD
UNIVERSITY PRESS

Great Clarendon Street, Oxford OX2 6DP

Oxford University Press is a department of the University of Oxford.
It furthers the University's objective of excellence in research, scholarship,
and education by publishing worldwide in

Oxford New York

Athens Auckland Bangkok Bogotá Buenos Aires Calcutta
Cape Town Chennai Dar es Salaam Delhi Florence Hong Kong Istanbul
Karachi Kuala Lumpur Madrid Melbourne Mexico City Mumbai
Nairobi Paris São Paulo Singapore Taipei Tokyo Toronto Warsaw

and associated companies in Berlin Ibadan

Oxford is a registered trade mark of Oxford University Press
in the UK and in certain other countries

British Library Cataloguing in Publication Data available
Library of Congress Catalog Card Number: 99–36900

ISBN 0 19 276224 9 (hardback)
ISBN 0 19 276257 5 (paperback)

Designed and typeset by Louise Millar

Cover illustration by Alison Jay, c/o The Organisation

Printed in Spain by Gráficas Estella, S.A.

The OXFORD TREASURY of CHRISTMAS POEMS

Michael Harrison and
Christopher Stuart-Clark

OXFORD
UNIVERSITY PRESS

Contents

The Twelve Days of Christmas

On the first day of Christmas
My true love sent to me
A partridge in a pear tree.

On the second day of Christmas
My true love sent to me
Two turtle doves, and
A partridge in a pear tree.

On the third day of Christmas
My true love sent to me
Three French hens,
Two turtle doves, and
A partridge in a pear tree.

On the fourth day of Christmas
My true love sent to me
Four colly birds,
Three French hens,
Two turtle doves, and
A partridge in a pear tree.

On the fifth day of Christmas
My true love sent to me
Five gold rings,
Four colly birds,
Three French hens,
Two turtle doves, and
A partridge in a pear tree.

On the sixth day of Christmas
My true love sent to me
Six geese a-laying,
Five gold rings,
Four colly birds,
Three French hens,
Two turtle doves, and
A partridge in a pear tree.

On the seventh day of Christmas
My true love sent to me
Seven swans a-swimming,
Six geese a-laying,
Five gold rings,
Four colly birds,
Three French hens,
Two turtle doves, and
A partridge in a pear tree.

On the eighth day of Christmas
My true love sent to me
Eight maids a-milking,
Seven swans a-swimming,
Six geese a-laying,
Five gold rings,
Four colly birds,
Three French hens,
Two turtle doves, and
A partridge in a pear tree.

On the ninth day of Christmas
My true love sent to me
Nine drummers drumming,
Eight maids a-milking,
Seven swans a-swimming,
Six geese a-laying,
Five gold rings,
Four colly birds,
Three French hens,
Two turtle doves, and
A partridge in a pear tree.

On the tenth day of Christmas
My true love sent to me
Ten pipers piping,
Nine drummers drumming,
Eight maids a-milking,
Seven swans a-swimming,
Six geese a-laying,
Five gold rings,
Four colly birds,
Three French hens,
Two turtle doves, and
A partridge in a pear tree.

On the eleventh day of Christmas
My true love sent to me
Eleven ladies dancing,
Ten pipers piping,
Nine drummers drumming,
Eight maids a-milking,
Seven swans a-swimming,
Six geese a-laying,
Five gold rings,
Four colly birds,
Three French hens,
Two turtle doves, and
A partridge in a pear tree.

On the twelfth day of Christmas
My true love sent to me
Twelve lords a-leaping,
Eleven ladies dancing,
Ten pipers piping,
Nine drummers drumming,
Eight maids a-milking,
Seven swans a-swimming,
Six geese a-laying,
Five gold rings,
Four colly birds,
Three French hens,
Two turtle doves, and
A partridge in a pear tree.

Traditional

Winter Days

Biting air
Winds blow
City streets
Under snow

Noses red
Lips sore
Runny eyes
Hands raw

Chimneys smoke
Cars crawl
Piled snow
On garden wall

Slush in gutters
Ice in lanes
Frosty patterns
On window panes

Morning call
Lift up head
Nipped by winter
Stay in bed

Gareth Owen

Winter

Winter crept
through the whispering wood,
hushing fir and oak;
crushed each leaf and froze each web—
but never a word he spoke.

Winter prowled
by the shivering sea,
lifting sand and stone;
nipped each limpet silently—
and then moved on.

Winter raced
down the frozen stream,
catching at his breath:
on his lips were icicles,
at his back was death.

Judith Nicholls

Before Christmas

The year tips, the sun
slips towards the sky's edge, and
dark bites at the day.

Shopping after dark:
hands clutching carrier-bags
stuffed with surprises.

The pillar-box's
smiling mouth swallows our cards,
cheered by the greetings.

Christmas cards snow through
the letter-box. Open them
and brightness thaws out.

Lying awake I
hear clattering hooves: reindeer
landing on the roof.

John Corben

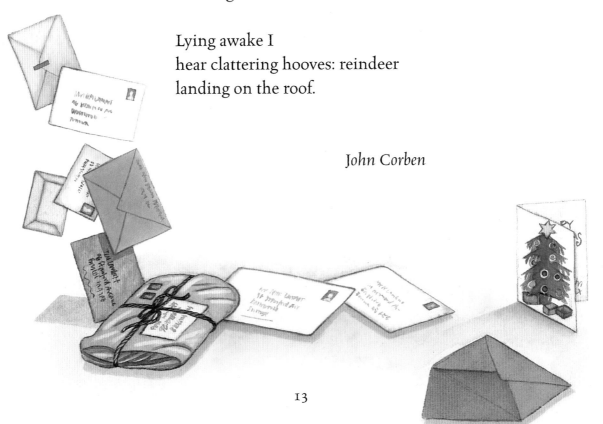

The Children's Carol

Here we come again, again, and here we come again!
Christmas is a single pearl swinging on a chain,
Christmas is a single flower in a barren wood,
Christmas is a single sail on the salty flood,
Christmas is a single star in the empty sky,
Christmas is a single song sung for charity.
Here we come again, again, to sing to you again,
Give a single penny that we may not sing in vain.

Eleanor Farjeon

Gabriel's Message

The angel Gabriel from heaven came,
His wings as drifted snow, his eyes as flame;
'All hail', said he, 'thou lowly maiden Mary,
Most highly favoured lady,
   Gloria!

'For know a blessèd mother thou shalt be,
All generations laud and honour thee,
Thy son shall be Emmanuel, by seers foretold.
Most highly favoured lady,
   Gloria!'

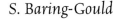

Then gentle Mary meekly bowed her head,
'To me be as it pleaseth God', she said,
'My soul shall laud and magnify his holy name.'
Most highly favoured lady,
   Gloria!

Of her, Emmanuel, the Christ, was born
In Bethlehem, all on a Christmas morn,
And Christian folk throughout the world will ever say,
'Most highly favoured lady,
   Gloria!'

S. Baring-Gould

Little Donkey

Little donkey, little donkey,
On the dusty road,
Got to keep on plodding onwards
With your precious load.
Been a long time, little donkey,
Through the winter's night.
Don't give up now, little donkey,
Bethlehem's in sight.

Ring out those bells tonight,
Bethlehem, Bethlehem.
Follow that star tonight,
Bethlehem, Bethlehem.
Little donkey, little donkey,
Had a heavy day,
Little donkey, carry Mary
Safely on her way.

Little donkey, carry Mary
Safely on her way.

Eric Boswell

16

Mary's Burden

My Baby, my Burden,
  Tomorrow the morn
I shall go lighter
  And you will be born.

I shall go lighter,
  But heavier too,
For seeing the burden
  That falls upon you.

The burden of love,
  The burden of pain,
I'll see you bear both
  Among men once again.

Tomorrow you'll bear it
  Your burden alone,
Tonight you've no burden
  That is not my own.

My Baby, my Burden,
  Tomorrow the morn
I shall go lighter
  And you will be born.

Eleanor Farjeon

Joseph and the Angel

As Joseph was a-walking, he heard an angel sing,
'This night shall be born our heavenly king.
He neither shall be born in housen nor in hall,
Nor in the place of Paradise, but in an ox's stall.
  Noel, Noel.'

As Joseph was a-walking, he heard an angel sing,
'This night shall be born our heavenly king,
He neither shall be clothèd in purple nor in pall,
But all in fair linen as wear babies all.
  Noel, Noel.'

As Joseph was a-walking, he heard an angel sing,
'This night shall be born our heavenly king.
He neither shall be rockèd in silver nor in gold,
But in a wooden cradle that rocks on the mould.
   Noel, Noel.'

As Joseph was a-walking, he heard an angel sing,
'This night shall be born our heavenly king.
He neither shall be christenèd in white wine nor in red,
But in the fair spring water, as we were christenèd.
   Noel, Noel.'

Traditional

Christmas Eve

Our mother was tearing her hair out,
(My sister and I played upstairs),
There was too much to do,
She would never be through,
And the air was quite blue;
So father had made himself scarce.

He'd been sent to do last-minute shopping
With a list as long as your arm.
Then to us mother said,
'You be useful instead,
Go and clear up the shed—
And leave me some peace to get calm!'

We put on our coats and our wellies
And moaned as we went through the door.
The thick cloud hung low,
And its strange, muddy glow
Held the promise of snow,
And the wind was quite biting and raw.

Our shed wasn't much of a building—
Its door had come off long ago.
What was once a tool-store
Now had cobwebs galore,
Fieldmice under the floor,
And corners where fungus could grow.

We piled things into the middle,
And on top of an old packing case
A basket was laid.
Then we propped up a spade,
Fork, and hoe as we made
A vain effort to tidy the place.

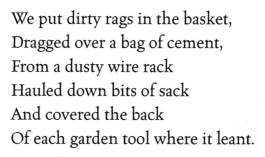

We put dirty rags in the basket,
Dragged over a bag of cement,
From a dusty wire rack
Hauled down bits of sack
And covered the back
Of each garden tool where it leant.

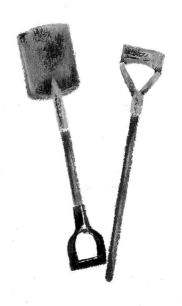

That evening the snow didn't happen,
The sky, full of stars, was aglow.
The moon shone its light
In the shed, and the sight
On that cold Christmas night
Made a wonder much greater than snow.

For it seemed a particular star hung
Just over the shed's wooden gable.
It silvered the floor
And the fine wisps of straw
So our old shed looked more
As if it were really a stable.

What we saw was a group of tall figures
Leaning over the cradle below.
A lamb knelt without sound,
And we looked all around
At the frost on the ground,
Hoping it might be snow.

Sandy Brownjohn

In the Week When Christmas Comes

This is the week when Christmas comes,
　　Let every pudding burst with plums,
And every tree bear dolls and drums,
　　In the week when Christmas comes.

Let every hall have boughs of green,
With berries glowing in between,
　　In the week when Christmas comes.

Let every doorstep have a song
Sounding the dark street along,
　　In the week when Christmas comes.

Let every steeple ring a bell
With a joyful tale to tell,
　　In the week when Christmas comes.

Let every night put forth a star
To show us where the heavens are,
　　In the week when Christmas comes.

Let every pen enfold a lamb
Sleeping warm beside its dam,
　　In the week when Christmas comes.

This is the week when Christmas comes.

Eleanor Farjeon

Christmas Morning

If Bethlehem were here today,
Or this were very long ago,
There wouldn't be a winter time
Nor any cold or snow.

I'd run out through the garden gate,
And down along the pasture walk;
And off beside the cattle barns
I'd hear a kind of gentle talk.

I'd move the heavy iron chain
And pull away the wooden pin;
I'd push the door a little bit
And tiptoe very softly in.

The pigeons and the yellow hens
And all the cows would stand away;
Their eyes would open wide to see
A lady in the manger hay,

If this were very long ago
And Bethlehem were here today.

And Mother held my hand and smiled—
I mean the lady would—and she
Would take the woolly blankets off
Her little boy so I could see.

His shut-up eyes would be asleep,
And he would look like our John,
And he would be all crumpled too,
And have a pinkish colour on.

I'd watch his breath go in and out.
His little clothes would all be white.
I'd slip my finger in his hand
To feel how he could hold it tight.

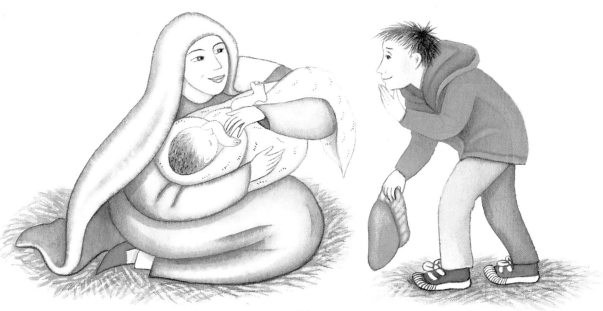

And she would smile and say, 'Take care',
The mother, Mary, would, 'Take care';
And I would kiss his little hand
And touch his hair.

While Mary put the blankets back
The gentle talk would soon begin.
And when I'd tiptoe softly out
I'd meet the wise men going in.

Elizabeth Madox Roberts

Little Jesus, Sweetly Sleep

Little Jesus, sweetly sleep, do not stir;
We will lend a coat of fur.
We will rock you, rock you, rock you,
We will rock you, rock you, rock you:
See the fur to keep you warm,
Snugly round your tiny form.

Mary's little baby, sleep, sweetly sleep,
Sleep in comfort, slumber deep.
We will rock you, rock you, rock you,
We will rock you, rock you, rock you:
We will serve you all we can,
Darling, darling little man.

trans. Percy Dearmer

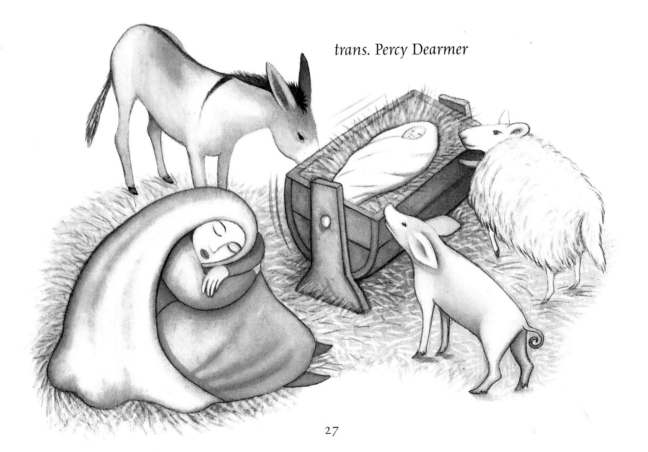

Lullaby, Jesus

Lullaby, Jesus,
My dear one, be sleeping.
Lullaby, Jesus,
While watch I am keeping.

Lullaby, baby,
My darling, I love you.
Your mother will sing
And so gently will rock you.

When you awaken,
Sweet Jesus, I'll give you
Raisins and almonds
And sweet berries too.

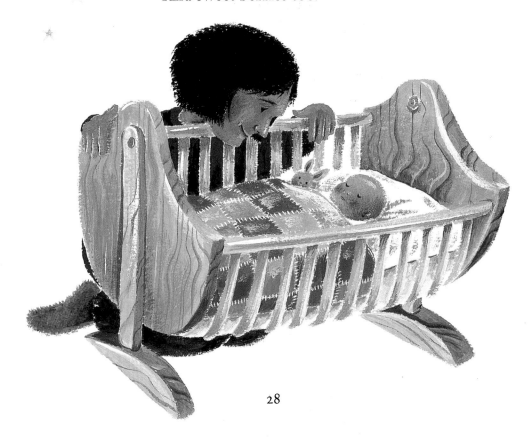

Lullaby, baby,
My darling, I love you.
Your mother will sing
And so gently will rock you.

Hush, he is sleeping
While stars shine above us;
Like the bright sun
Is the sweet baby Jesus.

Lullaby, baby,
My darling, I love you.
Your mother will sing
And so gently will rock you.

Traditional Polish

The Fir Tree

Oh! said the fir, still green with spring,
I don't get this worshipping
Of distant stars and a distant stranger
Wrapped in cloth in a fusty manger.

I can hold the stars each night
With my boughs, a winking light.
The crescent moon sits on my head.
Why not worship me instead?

Still, if you are set on Glory,
Let me be part of this story.
Take my boughs—a sweeter bed
You could not find to rest His head.

And let me stand up in the manger.
All my lights can ward off danger.
Green I stay—and so will He,
Throughout all eternity.

Jane Yolen

Winds Through the Olive Trees

Winds through the olive trees
Softly did blow
Round little Bethlehem,
Long, long ago.

Sheep on the hillside lay
White as the snow;
Shepherds were watching them,
Long, long ago.

Then from the happy skies
Angels bent low,
Singing their songs of joy,
Long, long ago.

For in his manger bed
Cradled we know,
Christ came to Bethlehem,
Long, long ago.

Traditional Gascon

Christmas Tree

Star over all
Eye of the night
Stand on my tree
Magical sight
Green under frost
Green under snow
Green under tinsel
Glitter and glow
Appled with baubles
Silver and gold
Spangled with fire
Warm over cold.

Laurence Smith

The Christmas Tree

They chopped her down in some far wood
A week ago,
Shook from her dark green spikes her load
Of gathered snow,
And brought her home at last, to be
Our Christmas show.

A week she shone, sprinkled with lamps
And fairy frost;
Now, with her boughs all stripped, her lights
And spangles lost,
Out in the garden there, leaning
On a broken post,

She sighs gently . . . Can it be
She longs to go
Back to that far-off wood, where green
And wild things grow?
Back to her dark green sisters, standing
In wind and snow?

John Walsh

The Christmas-tree Fairy

Here I am at the top of the tree,
Not as young as I used to be,
But doing my best—even if
My wings are torn and my joints are stiff
And my head is almost touching the ceiling—
To radiate the Christmas feeling.

This year they've put me out in the hall,
Squashed in the corner, close to the wall,
And a fearful draught from under the door
Keeps wafting my wand down to the floor.
Now, they've tied it on to my hand
With a far-too-tight, far-too-strong brown rubber band.

Last year, I thought they'd gone a bit far
When the eldest child wanted to put up a star!
But the father said, 'Yes, I know she looks jaded,
Her hair's lost its silver, her white dress has faded,
Her wings aren't so golden, her wand's a bit worn,
But we bought that fairy the year you were born!'

So here I am at the top of the tree,
Not the most comfortable place to be—
No one knows how the pine needles prickle,
No one would guess how the tinsel can tickle—
But while I'm up here, I know my place
And nothing can alter the smile on my face!

June Crebbin

Unable to Sleep

Unable to sleep,
I creep downstairs;
Nothing stirs
In this room-arrested darkness.

I pull the curtain
And peep through the window;
Frost, like a memory of snow,
Whitens my garden,
The roof of my neighbour's car,
The park beyond.

The coldness of winter covers my
Thoughts.

Behind me, the clock
Ticks into the ghost of time,
Ticks into my head,
Ticks into silence.

Peter Thabit Jones

Santa Claus

I *won't go to sleep*

Fur coat, fur hat, and fur-lined gloves,
And now he pulls his snowboots on.
His sledge is piled with sacks and sacks:
I'll wish again before it's gone.

I *won't go to sleep*

He walks the paddock deep in snow,
He harnesses his reindeer team.
The reindeer snort and shake their heads;
Their bells and harness-buckles gleam.

I WON'T *go to sleep*

Their comet rises through the air;
Fast-falling snowflakes pass them by.
With silent hooves and shaken bells
They stream across the starlit sky.

I . . . *won't . . . go . . . to . . .*

Clive Sansom

The Boots of Father Christmas

We're the boots of Father Christmas
And you ought to
Give more thought to
The boots of Father Christmas
When you're merry
With your sherry
For the boots of Father Christmas
Have a hard time
And a charred time
When the boots of Father Christmas
Land on raw coals—
Oh, our poor soles!

So the boots of Father Christmas
Ask you nicely,
But precisely:
Save the boots of Father Christmas
From our top hate—
A red hot grate,
Help the boots of Father Christmas:
When the sleigh's nigh,
Let the blaze die,
Then the boots of Father Christmas
Will be jolly
As your holly.

We're the boots of Father Christmas,
Please remember
Next December.

Richard Edwards

Dear Santa . . .

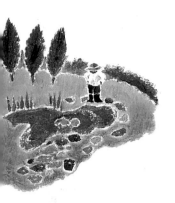

We're having our chimney extended
It's going to be very wide
You see, Jim wants a rhino for Christmas
And we'll never get it inside

We must make the fireplace bigger
Or Santa will really be sorry
For Dad wants a brand new back garden
While Grandma has asked for a lorry

A million-year-old hairy mammoth
Is what our young Hilda would like
Cousin Randolph has always been boring
He only wants a new bike

Mum's set her heart on a castle
With gas central heating all through
Aunty Madge prefers Buckingham Palace
Complete with a gold plated loo

We've written our letters to Santa
And this morning he gave us a ring
Says he'll post all our presents next Wednesday
Then he's off to Marjorca till spring.

Rita Ray

Questions on Christmas Eve

But *how* can his reindeer fly without wings?
Jets on their hooves? That's plain cheating!
And *how* can he climb down the chimney pot
   When we've got central heating?

You say it's all magic and I shouldn't ask
About Santa on Christmas Eve.
But I'm confused by the stories I've heard;
   I don't know what to believe.

I said that I'd sit up in bed all night long
To see if he really would call.
But I fell fast asleep, woke up after dawn
   As something banged in the hall.

I saw my sock crammed with apples and sweets;
There were parcels piled high near the door.
Jingle bells tinkled far off in the dark;
   One snowflake shone on the floor.

Wes Magee

The Man Who Steals Dreams

Santa Claus has a brother
A fact few people know
He does not have a friendly face
Or a beard as white as snow

He does not climb down chimneys
Or ride in an open sleigh
He is not kind and giving
But cruelly takes away

He is not fond of children
Or grown-ups who are kind
And emptiness the only gift
That he will leave behind

He is wraith, he is silent
He is greyness of steam
And if you're sleeping well tonight
Then hang on to your dream

He is sour, he is stooping
His cynic's cloak is black
And if he takes your dream away
You never get it back

Dreams with happy endings
With ambition and joy
Are the ones that he seeks
To capture and destroy

So, if you don't believe in Santa
Or in anything at all
The chances are his brother
Has already paid a call

Roger McGough

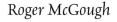

Blue Christmas

I'm having a lousy Christmas
Not even a robin in sight,
There's a great big hole in my stocking,
And I've just fused the Christmas tree lights.

The dog is away in the manger,
Even the pudding won't light;
Singing Merry Christmas
On this all-too-silent night.

Good King Wenceslas looked out
Over a year ago:
How can I follow his footsteps
When there isn't any snow?

The mistletoe's getting all dusty
With no one there to kiss,
Even the mince pies taste musty:
Can New Year be worse than this?

Adrian Henri

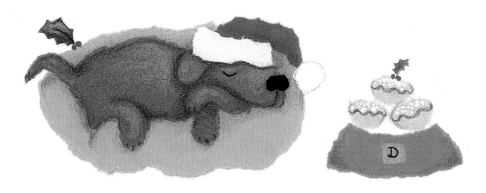

My Christmas : Mum's Christmas

decorations	climbing up to the loft on a wobbly ladder, probably falling.
a Christmas tree	pine needles and tinsel all over the carpet.
lots of food	preparations and loads of dishes to be washed.
crackers	crumpled paper everywhere.
presents	money down the drain.
sweets	indigestion and tooth-ache.
parties	late nights, and driving back through the dark.
snow to play in	getting soaked and frozen whenever outside.

Sarah Forsyth

The Wicked Singers

And have you been out carol singing,
Collecting for the Old Folk's Dinner?

Oh yes indeed, oh yes indeed.

And did you sing all the Christmas numbers,
Every one a winner?

Oh yes indeed, oh yes indeed.

Good King Wenceslas, and Hark
The Herald Angels Sing?

Oh yes indeed, oh yes indeed.

And did you sing them loud and clear
And make the night sky ring?

    Oh yes indeed, oh yes indeed.

And did you count up all the money?
Was it quite a lot?

    Oh yes indeed, oh yes indeed.

And did you give it all to the vicar,
Everything you'd got?

    Certainly not, certainly not.

Kit Wright

Xmas

I forgot to send
A card to Jennie—
But the truth about cousins is
There's too many.

I also forgot
My Uncle Joe
But I believe I'll let
That old rascal go.

I done bought
Four boxes now
I can't afford
No more, no how.

So Merry Xmas,
Everybody!
Cards or no cards
Here's HOWDY!

Langston Hughes

Christmas

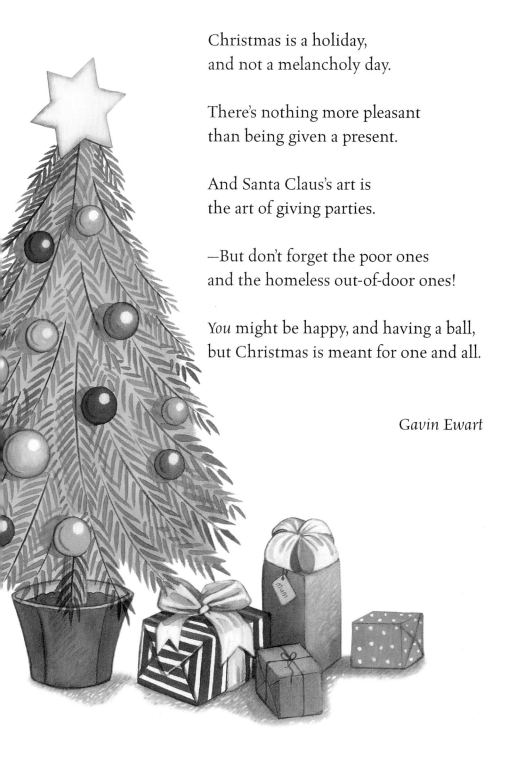

Christmas is a holiday,
and not a melancholy day.

There's nothing more pleasant
than being given a present.

And Santa Claus's art is
the art of giving parties.

—But don't forget the poor ones
and the homeless out-of-door ones!

You might be happy, and having a ball,
but Christmas is meant for one and all.

Gavin Ewart

Keeping Christmas

How will you your Christmas keep?
Feasting, fasting, or asleep?
Will you laugh or will you pray,
Or will you forget the day?

Be it kept with joy or prayer,
Keep of either some to spare;
Whatsoever brings the day,
Do not keep but give away.

Eleanor Farjeon

Come, See This Little Stranger

Come, see this little stranger
That lies all warm within;
His cradle is a manger,
His home a way-side inn;
Come, let us look within.

The breath of oxen warms him,
They watch this baby dear,
They see no chill shall harm him,
So long as they are near,
This little babe to cheer.

J. Steuart Wilson

Journey Back to Christmas

I ran to the church,
Ran all the way
With hay
From the pet shop
For our Christmas play.
I'd had to wait for the hay
And rehearsal was over. I was late.
Panting up the steps I heard the high church clock strike four—
They'd all gone!
I pushed the thick door
And was suddenly in
Quiet.
All the town's din
Gone.
One yellow light
Shone
Beyond the long, high, shadowy place
On a tablecloth with lace.
'That's the altar', our teacher'd said.
Now she saw me, smiled and called,
'Got the hay, Tim? Good. Now come and spread
It carefully about.'

She went out
And I was alone
In that big tent of stone.
It smelt of dust and flowers.
I walked along a lane between seats to the manger—
That wasn't the church's. That was ours.
We'd bought hardboard, made a trough,
Four legs of batten, sand-papered off—
The trough felt cold so I filled it with hay,
Warm hay, smelling of rabbits and summer,
I put more
On the floor
And wondered if that first Christmas Day
Was anything like our play—
Where Jesus is only a doll.

Was there a light
On Christmas Eve night
To show Mary and Joseph the way
When they were seeking a place to stay
In Bethlehem nearly two thousand years ago?
Was there snow?
Every little inn in Bethlehem that night
Was packed tight with strangers
And no one in any street
Could find a room or even a bed
To greet

Mary, whose baby—Jesus—would be born soon.
Was she afraid? Was there a frosty moon?
Then someone at last was able
To offer his stable.
Was he kind? Did he call his wife to help?
Had he a dog to snap and yelp,
Scenting danger
Because Joseph was a stranger?
Did the manger
In that stable smell as sweet as ours?
Did Mary's donkey push a grey-brown face
Into that manger?
I put mine in ours
And sniffed up ghosts of flowers—
I coughed and the sound
Went round and round in the shadows.
The church felt higher, full of darkness, cold and wide,
Miles from the street outside.

Under the light by the altar was a black chair.
I put it by the manger for Jean—
She's Mary in our play—she's fair.
And Joseph is Mark.
He's dark.
Were they really dark? or fair?
And was there a stool or chair
For Mary in that stable reeking of camels?
Was she frightened when the flickering lantern's light
Showed her—very close—a donkey's shining eyes, a cow's curled horn?
Did someone hold her hand until Jesus was born?

I put hay on the black seat
And more where Mary'd put her feet,
Some on the floor where she might lie.
Did the real Mary cry?
I stood back then to see
The whole scene where our play would be.
I act the part of a shepherd,
A young one,
Old Ezra's son.
And when the angels sing about God's son
Being born to Mary
I hear them first
And I call
To the others,
'Listen, all!
Hear the night sky burst
With joy
Because this boy,
God's son,
Is born today!'
I like saying that.
I like our play.
But I don't like the doll meant to be Jesus,
Pink and wrapped in a white sheet,
Tight and neat,
Still and flat.
Jesus wasn't like that!

Was he?
He was lively,
Soft, red, and wrinkled, very small,
With tiny toenails.
Did he kick and bawl
Till Mary wrapped him in her shawl?
Did she hear the shepherds whispering outside,
Cold feet, wrapped in hide,
Crouching on frozen mud?
I looked into the long dark of the church
And saw those shepherds—Well, I thought I did—
Saw them lurch
Against each other with tiredness,
There were six. There are six in our play.
A tall one, black-bearded, and his brother,
An old man and his son,
A round-faced one
And one other,

A boy like somebody I'd met.

The frost had melted on his coat;
His hair was wet.
He shook his head, looked up—and suddenly
I stood stone-still!
That boy I'd seen
Was me
—Or might have been—
I saw him smile and run and kneel at Mary's feet
On the hay I'd put by the seat.

'Please, lady, show us the King!
The angels sent us here—angels, lady.
We've come, hurrying.
Old Sam here's bust himself trying
To be first to greet your son.
Please, lady, I ain't lying.
I don't know much but I heard that singing!
We all heard it, didn't we? dong-dinging
It was—all clap-banging round the stars
Like bells and pipes and drums and bird calls
And all music. It made old Sam here dance.
It did, didn't it, Sam?
Show us the King, ma'am.
We never had much to bring
But we brought what we could
And that's all good.
Lady, show us the King.
God's son, the angels said
Though I don't see
How that can be,
You being ordinary
Though your face is sweet
Show us the King, lady.'

I saw and heard from where I stood,
Saw old Sam put out a hand, knobbly like wood,
And touch the boy's arm.

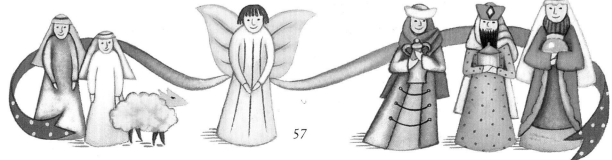

'Quiet, Tim. Be good.
He ain't a cheeky boy, ma'am.
He've brought ya a lamb,
His own,
Little black 'un—
Be a fine sheep when that's grown.
And here's cheese, coupla fleeces, and a goat skin.
—Hope that's all right—us comin' in.
You see the message was that you'd be here
Waiting with your baby to bring cheer
To us shepherds—and all men.
So we come immediately—Simeon, John, Ezra, Saul, and young Tim—
Couldn't leave him.
Said he had to see the King
So we let him come.
What's the baby's name, now, Tim?'
'Jesus. Mary, is that right?'
Mary nodded.

Then I saw old Sam
Pick up the baby on his arm
As he might a new lamb.

'I'll do him no harm, lady.
Little marvel, ain't ya!
You're the one the angels sang about.
Come and see the baby, Tim.'

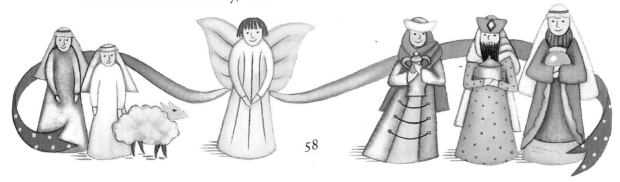

Then Tim—who looked like me—
Touched the baby.
I couldn't see
Jesus' face,
I wished I was in the boy's place.
I wished the baby in our play was real,
A real baby Jesus, alive and warm to feel.
Perhaps I'd understand
What son of God means
If I touched him with my hand.

The shadows swallowed the shepherds
My feet felt cold
Hay's not very warm on a stone floor.
I walked along that lane towards the door.
The clock wheezed overhead,
Ready to chime.

'Still here, Tim?
Do you know the time?
You must be cold.'

'You'd think they could have found
Something better than hay
For a new-born King
On a winter's day!'
From the door where we stood
We looked at the manger under the light—
'Yes, Tim, you would.'

Gwen Dunn

Away in a Manger

Away in a manger,
No crib for a bed,
The little Lord Jesus
Laid down his sweet head.
The stars in the bright sky
Looked down where he lay,
The little Lord Jesus
Asleep in the hay.

The cattle are lowing,
The baby awakes,
But little Lord Jesus
No crying he makes.
I love you, Lord Jesus;
Look down from the sky
And stay by my bedside
Till morning is nigh.

Be near me, Lord Jesus;
I ask you to stay
Close by me for ever,
And love me, I pray.
Bless all the dear children
In your tender care,
And fit us for heaven,
To live with you there.

Martin Luther

Nativity Play

This year . . .
This year can I be Herod?
This year, can I be him?
A wise man
or a Joseph?
An inn man
or a king?

This year . . .
can I be famous?
This year, can I be best?
Bear a crown of silver
and wear a golden vest?

This year . . .
can I be starlight?
This year, can I stand out?
. . . feel the swish of curtains
and hear the front row shout
'Hurrah' for good old Ronny
he brings a gift of gold
head afire with tinsel
'The Greatest Story Told . . .'
'Hurrah for good old Herod!'
and shepherds from afar.

So—
don't make me a palm tree
And can I be—
            a Star?

Peter Dixon

It Was Poor Little Jesus

It was poor little Jesus,
   Yes, Yes.
He was born on a Friday,
   Yes, Yes.
Didn't have no cradle,
   Yes, Yes.

   Wasn't that a pity and a shame,
   O Lord.
   Wasn't that a pity and a shame.

It was poor little Jesus,
   Yes, Yes.
The child of Mary,
   Yes, Yes.
He was laid in a manger,
   Yes, Yes.

   Wasn't that a pity and a shame,
   O Lord.
   Wasn't that a pity and a shame.

He was born on a Christmas,
   Yes, Yes.
He was born on a Christmas,
   Yes, Yes.
Didn't have no shelter,
   Yes, Yes.

   Wasn't that a pity and a shame,
   O Lord.
   Wasn't that a pity and a shame.

American Spiritual

Room at the Inn

Draughty, husband, that stable.
She looked . . . warm, though.
Almost at home.
And you know, husband, I swear
it's not one mite as dark in there
as you'd have thought.
And that child—so still, so quiet.
Perhaps they'll need more straw?
It won't get any warmer, early hours.
Maybe we should bring them in?
Husband, you're not listening!

There is our bed . . .
but then with breakfast early
and so many travellers . . .
Well, *they* won't go tomorrow, surely?
Husband, did you see . . . ?
Husband!
Oh well, old man, dream on!
Some day we've had,
and then those two arriving,
with every nook and cranny gone!

Funny how those moths
circled the old lantern,
husband. Almost like . . .
almost as if those three . . .
but no, it couldn't be!
And the light,
you should have seen the light!
Oh, it flickered, but
so bright, so bright,
and night so still.
Draughty it is, that stable,
husband.

Judith Nicholls

Mice in the Hay

out of the lamplight
whispering worshipping
the mice in the hay

timid eyes pearl-bright
whispering worshipping
whisking quick and away

they were there that night
whispering worshipping
smaller than snowflakes are

quietly made their way
whispering worshipping
close to the manger

yes, they were afraid
   whispering worshipping
as the journey was made

from a dark corner
   whispering worshipping
scuttling together

But He smiled to see them
   whispering worshipping
there in the lamplight

stretched out His hand to them
   they saw the baby King
hurried back out of sight
   whispering worshipping

Leslie Norris

In the Stable: Christmas Haiku

Donkey
My long ears can hear
Angels singing, but my song
Would wake the baby.

Dog
I will not bark but
Lie, head on paws, eyes watching
All these visitors.

Cat
I will wash my feet. For
This baby all should be clean.
My purr will soothe him.

Owl
My round eyes look down.
No starlit hunting this night:
Peace to little ones!

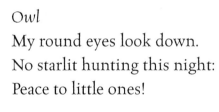

Spider
My fine web sparkles:
Indoor star in the roof's night
Over the baby.

John Corben

'I', Said the Donkey

'I', said the donkey, all shaggy and brown,
'Carried his mother all into the town,
Carried her uphill, carried her down.
I', said the donkey, all shaggy and brown.

'I', said the cow, with spots of red,
'Gave him hay for to rest his head,
Gave a manger for his bed.
I', said the cow, with spots of red.

'I', said the sheep, with twisted horn,
'Gave my wool for to keep him warm,
Gave my coat on Christmas morn.
I', said the sheep with twisted horn.

'I', said the dove from the rafters high,
'Cooed him to sleep with a lullaby,
Cooed him to sleep my mate and I.
I', said the dove from the rafters high.

Anon.

Cat in the Manger

In the story, I'm not there.
Ox and ass, arranged at prayer:
But me? Nowhere.

Anti-cat evangelists
How on earth could you have missed
Such an obvious and able
Occupant of any stable?

Who excluded mouse and rat?
The harmless necessary cat.
Who snuggled in with the holy pair?
Me. And my purr.

Matthew, Mark and Luke and John
(Who got it wrong,
Who left out the cat)
Remember that,
I was there.

U. A. *Fanthorpe*

The Christmas Mouse

A Christmas mouse
Came to our house,
Looking for crumbs
That clumsy thumbs
Had dropped on the floor.
Under the door
He quietly crept
And bits not swept
He nibbled and sniffed,
'A Christmas gift',
Old Mousie thought
And went and brought
His relations and friends
To share the ends
Of our Christmas feast.

Daphne Lister

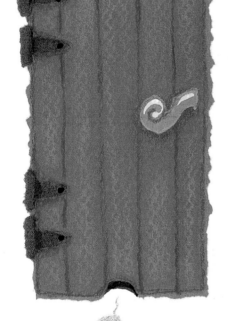

Oh, Who Would Be a Shepherd Boy?

Oh, who would be a shepherd boy
And mind a flock of sheep,
While other men and boys enjoy
A quiet night of sleep?

Yes, who would choose to pass the night
In darkness and in cold?
Or hear the cry without a fright:
'A wolf is in the fold'?

Now then there came a shining one,
An angel of the Lord;
With news of God's eternal son,
By angels now adored.

'The news', said he, 'should make you glad,
And fill your hearts with joy:
You'll find him in a manger laid,
A mother's baby boy.'

The shepherds' hearts were comforted
By what was told to them.
'And after what we've heard', they said,
'Let's go to Bethlehem.'

Traditional

Shepherds' Song

High in the heaven
A gold star burns
Lighting our way
As the great world turns.

Silver the frost
It shines on the stem
As we now journey
To Bethlehem.

White is the ice
At our feet as we tread,
Pointing a path
To the manger-bed.

Charles Causley

The Barn

'I am tired of this barn!' said the colt.
'And every day it snows.
Outside there's no grass any more
And icicles grow on my nose.
I am tired of hearing the cows
Breathing and talking together.
I am sick of these clucking hens.
I *hate* stables and winter weather!'

'Hush, little colt,' said the mare.
'And a story I will tell
Of a barn like this one of ours
And the wonders that there befell.
It was weather much like this,
And the beasts stood as we stand now
In the warm good dark of the barn—
A horse and an ass and a cow.'

'And sheep?' asked the colt. 'Yes, sheep,
And a pig and a goat and a hen.
All of the beasts of the barnyard,
The usual servants of men.
And into their midst came a lady
And she was cold as death,
But the animals leaned above her
And made her warm with their breath.

'There was her baby born
And laid to sleep in the hay,
While music flooded the rafters
And the barn was as light as day.
And angels and kings and shepherds
Came to worship the babe from afar,
But we looked at him first of all creatures
By the bright strange light of a star!'

Elizabeth Coatsworth

We Three Camels

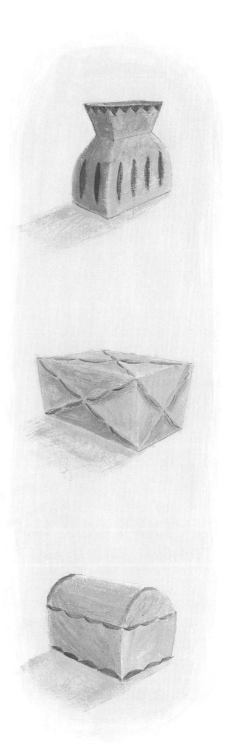

I carried a king,
But not the Child,
Through desert storms
And winds so wild
The sands crept into
Every pack.
But never did
My king look back.
'Forward!' he cried,
'We follow the star,
We do not stop.'
So here we are.

I carried a king,
But not the One,
Through searing heat
And blinding sun,
Through nights so cold
My nostrils froze,
And slaves wrapped
cloths
About my toes.
But forward we went
Led by a star.
We did not stop,
So here we are.

I carried a king,
But not the Babe,
And also boxes
Jewel inlaid.
My packs were stuffed
With scents and spice,
The grandest ladies
To entice.
No ladies saw we,
But only a star.
We did not stop
So here we are.

Jane Yolen

Counting Sheep

I am a poor shepherd.
Each sheep that lives the winter
is miracle enough for me.
That I have bread
and cheese and a skin
full of sweet wine on these cold hills
can pass for blessing.
So I will not say I was amazed
when angels thick as fleas
clustered in our meadow,
shouting hosannas that
frightened the sheep.

I lost two that night.
Still, a shepherd is not
so different from his flock.
We followed the bellwethers
to a rude manger
and crowded in amongst the cows.
What we saw then was miracle indeed:
a brand-new babe,
his unblemished face
shining in the light
of his mother's smile.

Jane Yolen

Children of Frost

Children of frost
children of snow
a long way to go to Bethlehem.

Children of dust
children of sun
the star told us to run to Bethlehem.

Out of the frost
out of the snow
we've brought a little fir tree to show to him.

Out of the dust
out of the sun
we've brought a baby camel to bow low
to him.

Holly sprigs
snow-laden twigs—

baskets of figs in our arms—

a sheet of ice
edelweiss—

    clusters of dates from our palms
    cardamom and cloves
    lemons from our groves—

sweet herbs to strew on his hay—

    some coral beads
    pomegranate seeds—

a rainbow we met on the way!

    Mary, come,
    show your son
    to all the children in Bethlehem.
    Hold him high,
    let him see
    all that our love can give to him.

Sue Cowling

The Snow

The snow, in bitter cold,
  Fell all the night;
And we awoke to see
  The garden white.

And still the silvery flakes
  Go whirling by,
White feathers fluttering
  From a grey sky.

Beyond the gate, soft feet
  In silence go,
Beyond the frosted pane
  White shines the snow.

F. Ann Elliott

Child's Carol

When there dawns a certain Star
　　Comes a Stranger into the city;
The feet of prayer his dear feet are,
　　His hands they are the hands of pity.

Every houseplace rich and poor
　　Shall show for welcome a sprig of green,
And every heart shall open its door
　　To let the Stranger enter in.

I will set my door ajar
　　That he may enter if he please;
The eyes of love his dear eyes are,
　　His brow it is the brow of peace.

Through the heart of every child
　　And man and woman in the city
He shall pass, and they be filled
　　With love and peace and prayer and pity.

Eleanor Farjeon

Christmas Thank Yous

Dear Auntie
Oh, what a nice jumper
I've always adored powder blue
and fancy you thinking of
orange and pink
for the stripes
how clever of you!

Dear Uncle
The soap is
terrific
So
useful
and such a kind thought and
how did you guess that
I'd just used the last of
the soap that last Christmas brought

Dear Gran
Many thanks for the hankies
Now I really can't wait for the flu
and the daisies embroidered
in red round the 'M'
for Michael
how
thoughtful of you!

Dear Cousin
What socks!
and the same sort you wear
so you must be
the last word in style
and I'm certain you're right that the
luminous green
will make me stand out a mile

Dear Sister
I quite understand your concern
it's a risk sending jam in the post
But I think I've pulled out
all the big bits
of glass
so it won't taste too sharp
spread on toast

Dear Grandad
Don't fret
I'm delighted
So *don't* think your gift will
offend
I'm not at all hurt
that you gave up this year
and just sent me
a fiver
to spend

Mick Gowar

Snowflake

Little shaving
of hot white cold
Snowflake
Snowflake
you really bold

How you feeling, Snowflake?
Icily-Hot
How you feeling, Snowflake?
Ice-Silly-Hot

Snowflake
Snowflake
you little clown

c
a
r
n
i
v
a
l
l
i
n
g
d
o
w
n

A small ghost kiss
on my warm tongue.

Grace Nichols

Snowing

Snowing. Snowing. Snowing.
Woolly petals tossed down
From a tremendous tree in the sky
By a giant hand, the hand
That switches on lightning
And tips down cloudbursts.
I like to think of it that way.

Quiet. Quiet. Quiet.
No noise of traffic in the street.
In the classroom only Miss Nil's voice
Dictating and the rustle of paper.
I am holding my breath in wonder.
I want to cry out 'Look! Look!'
Miss Nil has paused between sentences
And is looking out of the window.
But I suppose she is wondering whether
She'll have to abandon her car and walk home.

Snowing. Snowing. Snowing.
I wish I could go out and taste it.
Feel it nestling against my cheek.
And trickling through my fingers.
The message has come round we are to go home now
Because the buses may stop running.
So the snow has given us a whole hour of freedom.
I pick up fistfuls.
Squeeze them hard and hurl them.

But hurry, the bus is coming
And I want to get home early to look at the garden:
At the holly tree in its polar bear coat;
The cherries with white arms upstretched,
Naked of leaves; the scratchy claw marks
Of birds, and blobs of big pawed dogs.
And I want to make footprints of my own
Where the snow is a blank page for scribbling.
Tea time already. Still the snow comes down.
Migrating moths, millions and millions
Dizzying down out of the darkening sky.

Mother draws the curtains.
Why couldn't they stay open?
Now I can't watch the secretive birds
Descending, the stealthy army invading.
What does the roof look like
Covered with slabs of cream?
How high are the heaps on window ledges?
Tomorrow the snow may have begun to melt away.
Why didn't I look more
While there was still time?

Olive Dove

After Christmas

Darkness begins a
retreat: the cold light flows back
over the dead land.

Put the tree out now:
hang nuts on its branches—see feathered
decorations come.

Take down the Christmas
cards: arrowheads in the dust
point to spring cleaning.

Pull down the paper
chains: the room grows tall, the floor
deep in coloured snow.

Cold bites deep: warm your
mind at Christmas memories
and look for snowdrops.

John Corben

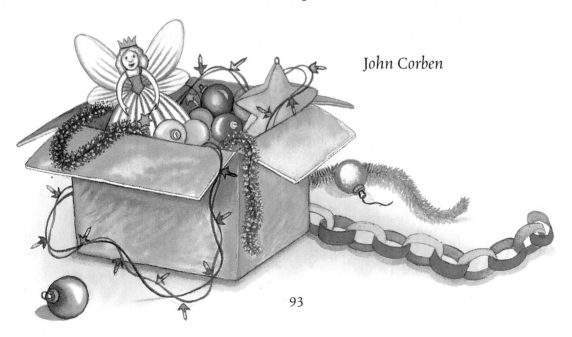

Index of Titles and First Lines

First lines are in italics

Index of Authors

Index of Artists

Acknowledgements

Eric Boswell: 'Little Donkey', words and music by Eric Boswell, copyright © 1959 Warner/Chappell Music, London W6 8BS, words reprinted by permission of IMP Ltd. **Sandy Brownjohn**: 'Christmas Eve' from *Both Sides of the Catflap*, reprinted by permission of the publisher, Hodder & Stoughton Ltd. **Charles Causley**: 'The Shepherd's Song' from *Collected Poems* (Macmillan), reprinted by permission of David Higham Associates Ltd. **Elizabeth Coatsworth**: 'The Barn' from *Compass Rose* (Putnam Publishing Group), reprinted by permission of Kate Barnes. **John Corben**: 'Before Christmas', 'After Christmas' and 'In the Stable: Christmas Haiku', all first published in Michael Harrison (ed.): *Junk Mail* (OUP, 1993), reprinted by permission of the author. **Sue Cowling**: 'Children of Frost' from *What is a Kumquat?*, reprinted by permission of the publisher, Faber & Faber Ltd. **June Crebbin**: 'The Christmas Tree Fairy' from *The Dinosaur's Dinner* (Viking, 1992), reprinted by permission of the author. **Percy Dearmer**: translation of 'Little Jesus, Sweetly Sleep' from *Oxford Book of Carols*, copyright © Oxford University Press 1928, reprinted by permission of Oxford University Press. **Peter Dixon**: 'Nativity Play' from *Big Billy* (Peche Luna Publications), reprinted by permission of the author. **Olive Dove**: 'Snowing' from *Drumming in the Sky* (BBC Books), reprinted by permission of the author. **Gwen Dunn**: 'Journey Back to Christmas' first published in M. Harrison and C. Stuart-Clark (eds.): *The Oxford Book of Christmas Poems* (OUP, 1983), reprinted by permission of the author. **Gavin Ewart**: 'Christmas' from *Like It or Not* (Red Fox) by permission of Mrs Margo Ewart. **Richard Edwards**: 'The Boots of Father Christmas' from *A Mouse in My Roof* (Orchard Books, 1988), reprinted by permission of the author. **U. A. Fanthorpe**: 'Cat in the Manger' from *Safe as Houses* (Peterloo Poets, 1995), copyright © U. A. Fanthorpe 1995, reprinted by permission of the publisher. **Eleanor Farjeon**: 'Child's Carol', 'Keeping Christmas', 'The Children's Carol', 'In the Week When Christmas Comes' and 'Mary's Burden', all from *Silver Sand and Snow* (Michael Joseph), reprinted by permission of David Higham Associates Ltd. **Sarah Forsyth**: 'My Christmas: Mum's Christmas' from *A Child's View of Christmas* (Exley Publications Ltd), reprinted by permission of the publisher. **Mick Gowar**: 'Christmas Thank Yous' from *Swings and Roundabouts* (Collins, 1981), reprinted by permission of the author. **Adrian Henri**: 'Blue Christmas' from *The Phantom Lollipop Lady and Other Poems* (Methuen Children's Books, 1986) copyright © Adrian Henri 1986, reprinted by permission of Rogers, Coleridge & White Ltd, 20 Powis Mews, London W11 1JN. **Langston Hughes**: 'Xmas' from *The Collected Poems of Langston Hughes*, copyright © 1994 by the Estate of Langston Hughes, reprinted by permission of the publishers, Alfred A. Knopf, Inc., and of David Higham Associates Ltd. **Peter Thabit Jones**: 'Unable to Sleep' from *A Christmas Stocking*, reprinted by permission of the publisher, Cassell plc. **Daphne Lister**: 'The Christmas Mouse' first published in *Gingerbread Pigs and Other Rhymes* (Transworld, 1980), reprinted by permission of the author. **Roger McGough**: 'The Man Who Steals Dreams' from *Pillow Talk* (Viking Penguin), copyright Roger McGough 1990, reprinted by permission of the Peters Fraser & Dunlop Group Ltd on behalf of the author. **Wes Magee**: 'Questions on Christmas Eve' from *The Witch's Brew and Other Poems* (Cambridge University Press, 1989), reprinted by permission of the author. **Judith Nicholls**: 'Winter' and 'Room at the Inn' both from *Midnight Forest*, reprinted by permission of the publisher, Faber & Faber Ltd. **Grace Nichols**: 'Snowflake' from *Give Yourself a Hug* (Puffin, 1994), copyright © Grace Nichols 1994, reprinted by permission of Curtis Brown Ltd, London, on behalf of the author. **Leslie Norris**: 'Mice in the Hay' from *Norris's Ark* (Tidal Press), reprinted by permission of the author. **Gareth Owen**: 'Winter Days' from *Salford Road* (Kestrel Books, 1979), copyright © Gareth Owen 1979, reprinted by permission of Rogers, Coleridge & White Ltd, 20 Powis Mews, London W11 1JN. **Rita Ray**: 'Dear Santa...' first published in Gary Boswell (ed.): *The Bee's Knees* (Stride), reprinted by permission of the author. **Elizabeth Madox Roberts**: 'Christmas Morning' from *Under the Tree*, copyright 1922 by B. W. Huebsch, Inc., renewed 1950 by Ivor S. Roberts. Copyright 1930 by Viking Penguin, Inc., renewed © 1958 by Ivor S. Roberts, reprinted by permission of the publisher, Viking Penguin, a division of Penguin Putnam, Inc. **Clive Sansom**: 'Santa Claus' from *The Golden Unicorn*, reprinted by permission of the publishers, Methuen Children's Books (a division of Egmont Children's Books Ltd). **Laurence Smith**: 'Christmas Tree', first published in M. Harrison and C. Stuart-Clark (eds.): *The Oxford Book of Christmas Poems* (OUP, 1983), reprinted by permission of the author. **John Herbert Walsh**: 'The Christmas Tree' from *Poets in Hand* (Penguin Books) reprinted by permission of Patrick Walsh. **John Steuart Wilson**: words of 'Come, See This Little Stranger', reprinted by permission of Oxford University Press. **Kit Wright**: 'The Wicked Singers' from *Rabbiting On* (Collins, 1978), reprinted by permission of the author. **Jane Yolen**: 'The Fir Tree', 'Counting Sheep' and 'We Three Camels', copyright © 1991 by Jane Yolen, first published in *Hark! A Christmas Sampler* (G. P. Putnam's Sons, New York), reprinted by permission of Curtis Brown Ltd, New York.